# taj chander

# GRAiL

poems

*GRAIL* by Taj Chander

FIRST EDITION, Copyright © 2024 by Taj Chander

Published in the United States by Great Moon Books
Memphis, TN



Library of Congress Control Number: 2024917916

ISBN 979-8-218-98489-2

Cover Design & book layout by TC

Subjects: Poetry, Spirituality

Printed in Collierville, TN

Dedicated to the practitioners

Does anyone understand why we're all here having a human experience? Please explain. Thank you.

👍 Like          💬 Comment          ↪ Share



**Still searching** 👍

# Foreword

The concept of this book began shortly after visiting The Pyramid of the Sun, Teotihuacan, Mexico in 2017. I attended an Aztec sweat ceremony that seemed to set in motion the events of the next seven years of my life. Upon returning to the states I had been working as a mostly angry artist and professor. I attended a viewing party for what was called the "Great American Eclipse." On that sweltering August day in Louisiana, in a wash of crescent-moons beneath the live oaks a shift occurred shaking me to the very foundation of my being, changing everything I thought I knew about my life's trajectory. The following months resulted in a series of mysterious departures from nearly every idea I had of my personal identity. It was a cusp-era, a Saturn return, a series of divorce, loss of occupation, collaborative partnerships, and sense of home. There was death, upheaval and un-trust. It was the end of what I thought was "my life's work." I was at a crossroads between my conceived self and *'the truth'* of who I am.

These poems represent a self-portrait in four cities— the terminus points along *El Camino Real, a* colonial trail system crossing the borders of the United States and Mexico, all of which represent places lived, loved, hurt, made art, toiled, learned and honed, from the Deep South to Silicon Valley. What later revealed itself to me was a symbolic path toward a higher realization. What I was reckoning with was the reconciliation between the borders of my body and soul, identity and infinity, the so-called new age and old-time religion on a fundamental level. What I'm trying to say is: through the upheaval, the road took me through a nearly indescribable self-experience toward, dare I say, a path of higher destiny.

The pandemic was when I met my teachers. I was fortunate to work privately with Ariana Reines' through her digital poetry salon: *Invisible College*, where I also met my Kundalini Yoga teacher, tanner menard. It was this synthesis paired with daily practice, meditation and study in which GRAIL became a notebook in making meaning of the many suns and moons along *The Road.*

# CONTENTS

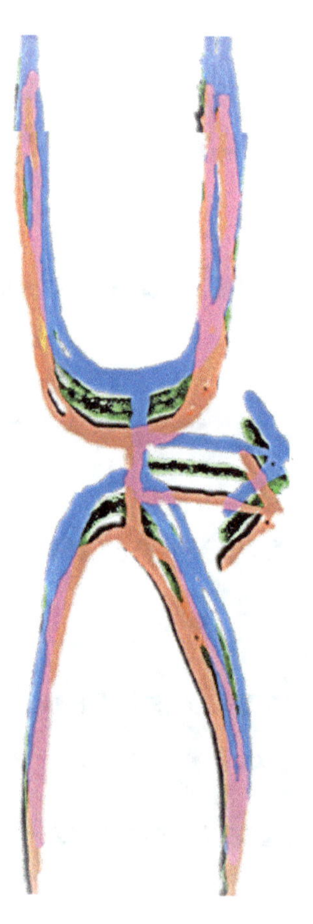

"Let he who seeks not cease until he finds,
And when he finds, he will be astonished"

-Gospel of Thomas

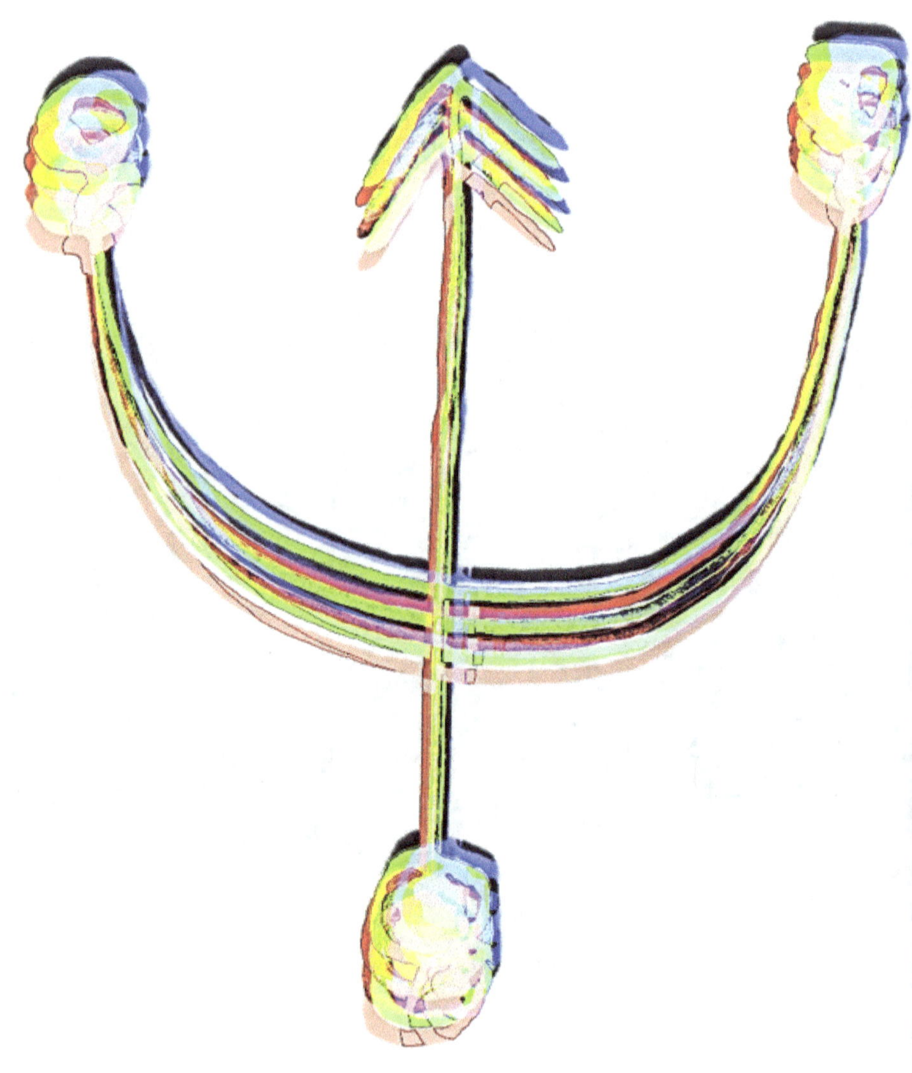

# GLIMMER

Sometimes when
I move my eyes up
The screen
Reading Gmail

I see Grail

How many miles
My fingers have
Scrolled

Touching my words
Illumines a screen
Machine traced to my crown

Down my veins, time hurling
The planet turns our fractal faces

I do not know how to exist
But still I am existing

The math speaks
What the heart is full of

Long before my eyes averted
I knew I'd been subconsciously
Taken, by the image
And it's light, I was darkening
From a vision not my own
Saying nothing of the nearsighted
Nature of my eyes from donating
So much of them to the initial and related
Inventions of my generation

There was a grey depression building
From the static memories of people
And their bodies pixellating
Everyone was losing sight in the distortion
The jump-cuts and hashtag movements
The stories deconstructed, the code that
By the time had reached our eyes became
A light, a language calculated
like an abacus, like a zodiac

The shape of things we carried was shrinking
It was changing what we could remember
It knew more than we did about ourselves
People were becoming numb to the machinations
And besides, memory was getting expensive
Biometrics and automation, a transmogrification
A mixed reality, a Jacquard fabric
But the fabric was us, and the programming
Of the language became the reality itself

It caused a creeping accuracy, evolving
Alongside the war, people couldn't describe it anymore
In predictive text, no one had time to find the correct
Words, automatic weapons and mineral intelligences advanced
The error — it was fixed, a convenience, a maintenance, a taking

It was written in the scroll, etched upon a mirror
Causing giant holes in the collective aura
Like the Buddhist "wound with nine holes"
But it was only when you committed a crime that
The wound was pieced together, backwards into
A portrait of yourself, digital ruins composing
A sophisticated realism, a cinematic echo of
Everything ever volunteered in fun or fury

Don't speak or sneeze but yet the ether was becoming
Crowded with currencies, pornography and popular opinion
Everywhere disorder was being classified as a qualification
You weren't allowed to say, you weren't allowed, what went
unspoken was felt in more subtle realms

At the crossfire of awareness
The sport of virtue
Signaling a cruel performance
And everything was being recorded

The human hand reaching
Closer to the advent
Searching for what's equal
To secrets scratched on papyrus

Fingerprints smeared on glass

Binary beings, eyes gleaming
For touch. Touch yearns—
Yearns for the ancient drum

Under electric clouds, the sound
Between bodies, a system
Superhuman, supernatural

A fire's warmth
The past murmuring
A present gap

Mudra to mudra
With the earth. Move—
Through the pulse of time

The planet's veins
Sing the velocity

## Fault

I know that many people would not be proud
to say *I am American*.
Though, I am— not in esteem, but as one
resting on the earthquake.
I know it stands.
It can stand everything but it's own beauty.
It can stand everything but "our" own.
And our own can stand everything but being
us.

(Great American Eclipse, April 2024)

# VESSELS

# Dream — 10/10/10

In catacombs of memory, I was
Wrestling with my father, tears were
On my lover streaming, in the grass
With my mother, falling into the gap
Between moments expiring and
Arising, as the owl asked its question
Luminous & empty, the night falling
In glittering pieces, I left
The door open, sirens
Rang through the city

I don't know who I am

# First Memory of Sun

Windowpane—
History of light, once.
Tree, maybe tall, leaves spread—
Before or after.

That silhouette, familiar—
Shadow. Past or— Glimpse
Ahead. The space between
Birth, rebirth.

Blades, a faded spring.
Did they ever know?
Death's question— Was it ours
Universal— Unanswered.

Vintage sun—
Era lost.
Blade-walk.
Blade-edge.
Blur, Sun-cut.
Tree-glass.

# House on American Plains

The house on American plains
stood, a silhouette against memories of sunlit rain
Each brick held more
than mortar—
bankruptcy's hand that gripped tight
death's hush on a still night
and the ugly scars
of divorce's divisive farce.

Old albums digitized
on cloud where past lies, swipe
to remember the creak
of floorboards, or the ember
glow of the fireplace.

Here, the horizon seemed to bend
with the weight of endings,
and beginnings.
in the same breath—
flesh and blood scattered,
a constellation undone
still by invisible thread,
they seek each other
in the vast digital night.

In the cold glow, they trace
the home they knew,
and in the absence,
in the quiet spaces between messages— resonance.

On the edge of a new strain
of consciousness, the pain
is palpable,
But so is the pull
of shared history with kin,
of that house on the plains,
monument in the mind—a nexus

Unyielding,  Unchanged,  Unending

## Memoriam

When funerals and showers
Were moved online

I went to the internet
And found you had died

I scrolled to the end
Where it said you were born
Again in this pixellated
Mausoleum

Preserved in your best
*Guide your way on*
*Guide your way on*
*Guide your way on*

This creeping comes
Like a tooth turning grey
What I gave of myself
To give myself away

Tell me you're not a robot
Have a cookie
You may get lonely
In this book
Of constellations

I'm reaching out
The window of my machine
Eyes pierce the screen
Of who I am

If I die
May history show
My search was not made in vain

# Hurricane

Cardboard boxes of our house
The room still haunts me after lightning
Cracked my screen we touched
Ourselves over the phone

We wrecked

# Message in a Bottle

There were rumors
He broke his sobriety
In the quarantine hotel
Last holiday weekend

The sun didn't shine
Two weeks straight

I was missing home
When Mom told me
She knew the perfect cocktail
For when I start drinking again

I keep saying
I'm a human being
Human, doing
This hangover from
The age of reason

Where truth is like a bullet
& hits harder than liquor

# 40 Days

I was told to write
"If I were not afraid"
Whatever that may be

I must have agreed in principle
It was spilling from my pen
A fury rushing in from another life

The next step:
Circling a special few
To scratch and write I WILL

I draw a box
From corner to corner
Obliterating my blocks

Then folding it
Into a tiny pyramid
The end of the exercise

Later, I think about intention
The artifact I keep measuring
The progress changing me

What did I write
In those deep blue lines
Of ink at tantric angles

Hermetically sealed
By these hands
That have done so much harm
To myself

I walked toward the church
Didn't know where else to go
Surveillance cameras blinking
Through the colors of the firmament
The drifter on the steps was whistling
The Hallelujah Chorus— trains were
Howling in A Major— lack of trust

(January 2018)

QUEST

# Siri

Make a slight right
Turn down the 99

Find the 1 you afraid of being lost
Before the light was
turned to time and
priced—

Our phones — our satellites
stars and inner faith
An *interface* — 'a brand'
of travel

Sol — the sole proprietor
Where do the breadcrumbs go?

And where does the sun go at night and will it return?
And where does a person go when they die?
And where does a person come from?
And how will I hold and bear witness
To the true heights and depths of my experience?
And how does one bear this consciousness?

# Cloud

<u>Memory</u>

    —> Filter >

            Brighten
            Add Significance
            Warp…
            Shift Blame
            Edit Lies
            Replace Intent
            Find Meaning
            Adjust Emotion
            Saturate
            Soften Errors
            Actualize
            Resize

             ^ ^
              ^ ^
               ^ ^
                ^ ^
               +

((ma)(N)(ra))

# Decryption

*(After the 1984 Macintosh Super Bowl Commercial)*

in a world of bald men

one Hooters waitress
smashes the screen

and the human
drones are showered
in the light

# End of History

Mushroom clouds are legal
Psilocybin is not

I look toward my screen
And already I forgot

Akashic records
Described as graffiti
On bathroom walls

What happened to America
Was inscribed inside
The toilet stall

Searching for the answer
To prove I wasn't wrong

*Dear God*
*Please let there be*
*No internet*
*In the beyond*

**Read** 1:11 PM

# I Remember MapQuest

Five fingers with a scrap of map
Scratched onto the palm

Inside our mother's ocean
Rushing through her shore's
Terrain of touch

Our hands have lines
Connecting us
If we look close enough

# Tik-Tok

I downloaded the app
 bc the president
  was banning it

But the culture war
 in my phone
  became hypnotic

Watching
 missiles fly
  on Tik-Tok

Tik-Tok

Tik-Tok

Tik-Tok

# Half Moon


Flag half-staffed at the Winchester Mansion
Hailing contemporary priced mortgages
On the brink of extinction 100 years later
90 seconds to midnight, a moment of silence
A seance bell concerning the specific spiritual consequence
Involving our inheritance of the gun — palms spreading
Across the asphalt, three signs reading:

Century 21

Century 22

Century 23

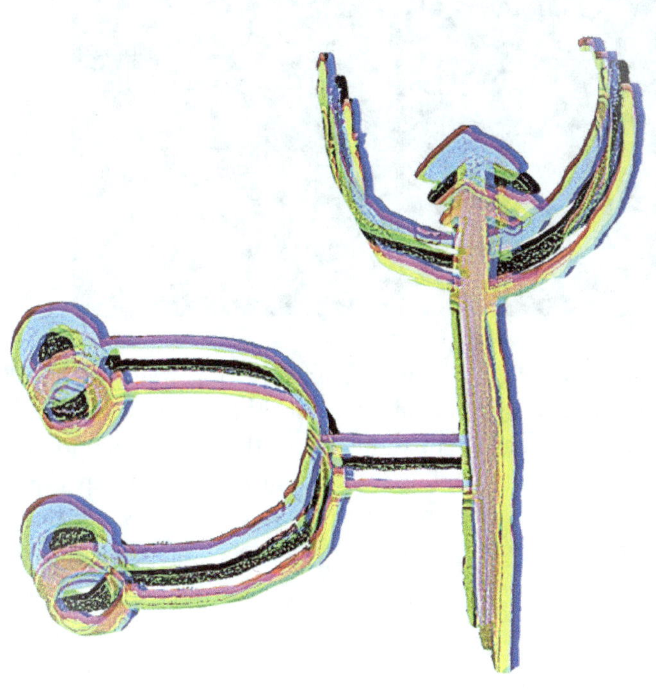

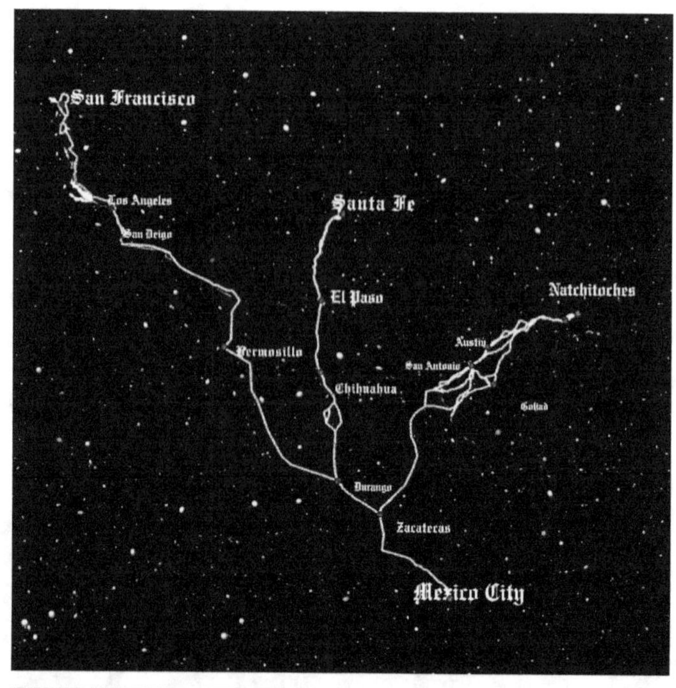


The "Camino Real" or "King's Highway" is a system of roads that were utilized by Spanish Colonists in the 16th and 17th centuries to connect the missions across the continental interior. Many of them originated by Indian footpaths. Some say the El Camino Real is a forerunner of the interstate highway system in the present day United States and Mexico.

*Kim Kardashian wearing tan*
*Cracked & disintegrating into pockets*
*Fading to the sound of conversation*
*Awakened to Hugh Jackman on pause*
*And everyone gone in a parking lot*
*Tents and scorched hills of Stockton*
*Behind the Family Dollar*
*Employees on the curb, blurry in the fumes*
*Officers searching for human traffic*
*On a bus with my baggage*
*Shattering my dream of California.*

(Greyhound Bus, October 2019)

# CAMINOS

today, fortunate

what am I searching for?

today, desolate

what am I searching for?

today, compassionate

what am I searching for?

today, impatient
what am I searching for?

deeper mystery

what am I searching for?

weight of history

what am I searching for?

incomprehensible–

what I searching for?

material, spiritual

what am I searching for?

behind the hysteria
what am I searching for?

in the unbearable
what am I searching for?

today, shareable

what am I searching for?

today, comparable

what am I searching for ?

virtue of telephony

what am I searching for?

the wireless fidelity
what am I searching for?


again and again


what am I searching for?
I am, I am

what am I searching for?

## Golden One

Money makes the world go round

      like a coin that spins midheaven

# Algorithm

Living life within the lines
But further from the heart

The confines of an income
The patterns of a job

The hardening of service
To wages taxed by war

Within these lines of vision
Are the limits of our love

# Road Opener

The road of redemption — set me free

The road of damnation — abandoned me

The road of ruin — helped me see

The road is human — help me please

The road of anguish — where I learned to grieve

The road of language — where I was naive

The road of corruption — the scheme I believed

The road is a junction —  a skeleton key

The road of connection — routes like a tree

The road of reflection — a ceremony

The road to home — haunting me

*It's a hard highway to travel for a soul in a body*

# New Mexico, Highway 106

The desert road at night unfurls

It flexes like the cat then curves

Towards the cows and sagebrush

Driving fast with windows down

The ashram glitters in the moonlight

Venus centered just above my lover

I'm trying to decide if this is what I want

# Cash Cow

When Jack threw beans
On a mound of dirt
It cracked the seed
Unfurled the root— spun
Golden  rainbow roe

The colors of an empire
Burned October's flame
As Moses swept the mountain
Red sun moved in warm montage

How much the cost of scorned earth
Worth her weight in gold
How much the cow to get into heaven

Giant questions like:

How long

Will we

Have food

# Living In My Car

Under the influence of a meme
I was unforgiving
Replaying the same stories
Only part of me was living

In my car I thought—
My life was insignificant

Another lover with a lighter
Turned into ashes, left behind me

Where the sofa used to be

# Prosperity Gospel

I was standing at the crossroads
It was the crossroads of my life
Where it demanded that I dance
Rule, indict— it rippled
In the wind, it's striped skin
Like a snake, it hissed
Not alive but living
At the threshold
Where I was inside

Seductive
How it folds
Like cloth, to paper
Shell to fur
To feather, down
Into the nest—
What was before
The concept— gift

Do you remember
What it meant
To take the reigns—
The weight of being

It was mine— iridescent
Silence on the water
Air on the night shift
Breathing during rest

Was this where discretion vanished?
Rights were gone — No
Choices left.

Choosing came
With consequences capitalized
Consumed, condemned
As community became a bought thing
Commodified, keeping occupied — Spent
As time kept healing, telling, killing

Don't cough
So many hands have
Folded, crumpled,
Changed, tossed, pinched
Held tightly in their fingertips
Virtual fingerprints
Lifts from glass
Cleaned to never be
Seen or held again
We signed our name to this
In the pillar of the sun
In the coffeeshops at dawn, there
"i" and the pen I clutched did— it flowed
Into the liquid screen
iHold

It feels so long since I've been home
Have you?  When
Could you feel it coming to an end—
The dream

It seemed like nothing stalled, the jobs
Fell into the deep, a sleep
So rich you couldn't wake
You couldn't shake yourself

It's like a jail, a school of light
Lessons written on the skin
I offered mine to breathe
Each breath changing me
Exchanging— rise and fall
Inscribed into a memory
Life's worth—  valuing

I look into your eyes, trying to time in
Do you really want to be born again?
Here? — counting fingers, hair, teeth, lines
On skin, what's left of me — you
You — leaving remnants of decay
You — In the corridors of time
like gospel being played

The heart left hungry
In the cracking temples
The money throwing itself out
Day after tedious day


The nature of the road goes on
This could still be the holy place


De$tiny

I cannot say exactly
What I've spent
My lifetime chasing

But how insane it is
To leave — where one arrives
The inverse of my wandering
Where I call myself
An identity

Imminently going off
Like eyes toward a screen
Like bombs into the now—
The world blown up— inflation
This expansion in between
Where I am here
With you


We must
Believe

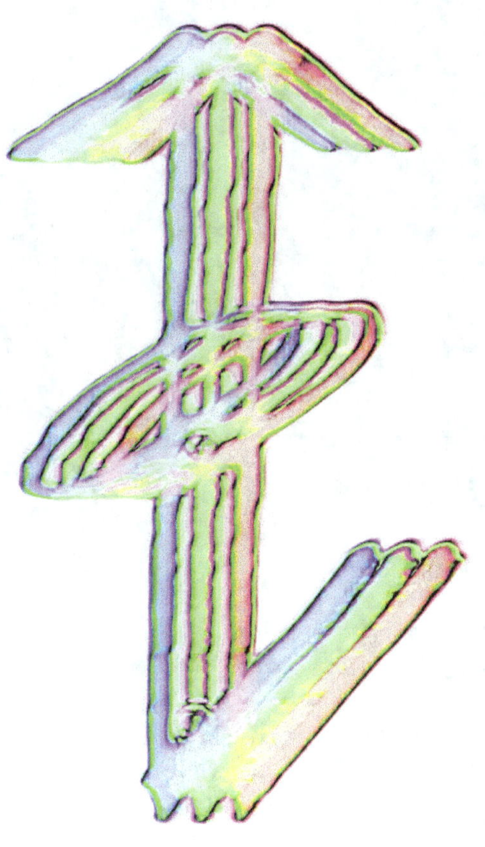

## Inner Apostle

I feel the closest to God where I can
Reach out and help. It is here I can
Help feed the hunger and they come
For the feeding and God provides.
Sometimes, I need encouraging here
On the roadside. If you're lost, just say,
"I need something to eat, I'm hungry." "Give me a drink."
And it's just that simple, Matthew. What you do
For the least of them, in unexpected ways. I do
All I can do.

(Sister J. Leonard, Summer 2016)

# SANCTUARY
# POEMS

# Echo

the first creation
 was  a  sound
which spoke
a light into the world


  the  first
   Sun    edged                    the moon's
      frequency as lightning          emblems
       coursed  through
        my  veins


      life  hidden              as  the child seeks
       beneath the rocks          the  answer  to
       how  far  a               wounds
        light bounces before         becoming unseen
       it fades


      phenomenon tells us            this living pillar will  fall
     that  we  are                 petrifying into stones
    loose against the veil             for  living  worms
      while  the channelers
       tell  us  the same things             to  heal
       as  a medium once told  me
       the hedge was shredded              to  remember
     what isn't  good  enough


     mere pockets  of limited  change

## The Unquestioned Answer

When he asked me what key this place was in
I thought I heard B-flat, the pitch at which
Medieval men once thought the earth was shaped.

Some still think that the earth is an image;
Centerfold tacked up on a wall, while the
Physicists at CERN make little black holes.

Schumann resonance off the charts today.
Nobody knows what the truth really is,
Except that when you hear it, you just know:


What is the closest one can be to God

A
dove
ascends
from the
sounds
of sirens
trucks & trap music
a remedy coo'd deep in the soul, soothes
the mood, she sings the blues:
on a sizzling wire
summer high
of one
o' nine
degrees
she knows,
she sings, she
mourns—she knows
she's seen this all before
she knows she's seen
this all before

# Every Surge— Ocean

Water within, more than
Quench or flood

Cascade
Of liquid timelines

Resurface
Deep within the bark—

When skies held no allure
When thirst was all we knew

Hold a leaf—
It's thrum

Every rain
Archived

We are both

Chronicler
Record

Under the
Canopy

Shining
Leaf

Veiled
Eons

Sunlight

Forest floor

# Hologram

*"just let it happen"*

pulsed the harlequin entity

against my frontal lobe


I couldn't un-hear it

beneath the moss

a sapphire luminescence


of earth into water

dissolved into fire

into air into ether


*"window within mirror"*

in the Jupiter silence

forest creatures

held their breath

# Resonance

suspended in the maw of dreamtime

sleeping prophets wake to sound

the gong of hearts in rhyme

as the past two-thousand years

begins to flow into infinity

# Slay

I see the fire rising and become
All living water I feel
The breathing I do not know
How long the sound I blast
The beam held to Infinity

I hear the fire whining and I listen
Where it simmers as I follow it
Into my coiled veins

Inside the thought
Forms fall— the dance
You really can forgive them
In their bleeding

Holding steady
Find the main road—
Self-created

/\
/\
/\

*Tonight inside a sanctuary*
*With those I love in silence*
*In this holy place, this night*
*Sounds of ambulance tonight*
*Season's first and final days as*
*I write these words tonight, I'm*
*Lighting candles quiet as your*
*Grief   meets   mine   tonight*
*Portal lights are making music*
*Place  of  open  doors  tonight*
*I thought I heard a mother sigh*
*As blue lights pierced her eyes*
*Because we're waiting in a line*
*And so the labyrinth takes me in*
*I know I shouldn't have but did*
*I  thought  of  loneliness  again*
*I make my plans, know they will change*
*As the stars change every night over street*
*Lamps shining copper bright remembering those*
*Lonely nights, another night, this very night, tonight*
*Within the silence,   sounds of ambulance,   tonight*

## Silent Prayer

In these days

Filled with images

Give me eyes to see

Into the shadows

Cast by pixels

Ears to hear beyond

The shots left ringing


Soften the blows

Through these vast waves

Of information

If I am to sleep

Let there be peace

Liberation

In the realm of dreams


May emptiness be

A vessel to recognition

As I wake to know

The deepest silence

As the healer's language

# Vela

In the blue screen cold

Of this waking hour

Night weighs over me


I gaze and I know

And you know

We knew these paths


Shooting stars bend

Toward the chasm's dust

Time measures itself in circles


There is an epic nothing between

What is and was and will be,  and how

We find our way to one another

My fire is a voice
My back is a bridge
For the soul to pass over
For the soul to pass over

(sun gazing, May 2022)

# EVENSONG

there is a song that wants to sing itself through me


through every poem and whisper

about reality and God


I could not sing this song

without time and grief

which brought me here


wanting peace

my hands reaching

through those of the cave painters

basket makers and weavers

artisans and healers

connected through the ages

within this cathedral

of the human condition

this song may be

a requiem or a song of rebirth

orchestrated through humankind's greatest

moral strength and determination


I don't know how this will play out


but I learned not to pave it over

that my denial and apathy is my own

my own difficulty looking

at what I have done

across right & wrong

between good & bad

most days I don't feel bad

enough for my dad


in the hymns of Saint Francis: "this is my father's world"


in the songs of Bill Monroe: "this world is not my home"

in the fog of sickness

in the fog of war

in the fog of bombs

and e.m.f. waves

and information overload


there is a great hole in my life that opens up

as a child in the fields
what felt so visceral and real

gave me a sense that
the world was very wise
and intelligent

gave me an appetite
to disappear into it

a fire that made
the summer so vivid

my biggest fear
was the world ending

afraid to look at the news app
on the verge of nuclear war


when something rearranges
the furniture of my mind
and suddenly I realize

I'm not climbing up Jacob's ladder anymore

but that God has been here the entire time

as God becomes the earth and speaks

to the earth, I am called

not to run from the fear

the outrage

the discomfort

but to look at it

to breathe it

and see it's turning

revealing

it's other face

the other face

of my pain for the world

which is my love for the world

the inseparable

world as lover

world as self

when the world itself becomes sacred

the constrictions

that my culture

has made

around God

fall away

like dried crusts

nectar on my forehead— I merge

to become that which I love

THE SQUARE
ROOT OF VICTORY
IS THY
SELF

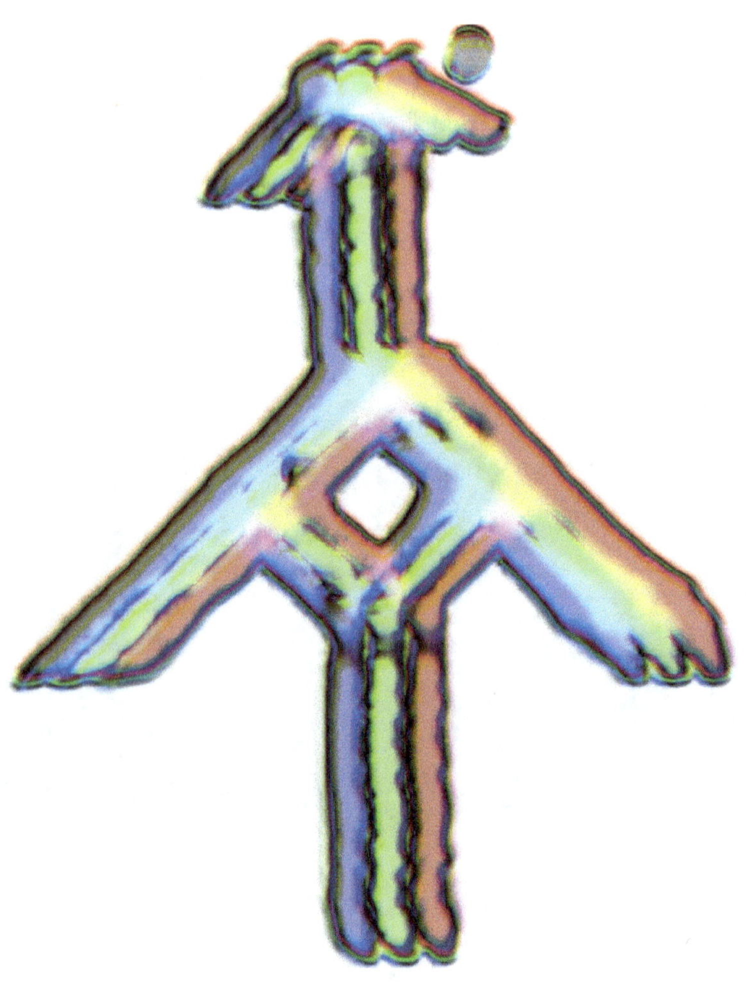

what's coming

is all that's left

<u>Acknowledgements</u>

Special thanks to my teachers:
Ariana Reines, Tanner Menard, & Madra Little

With additional love to friends and colleagues for their support and inspiration: Vivian Giourousis, Stephen and Emily Guenther, Carly Nguyen, Cristy Michel, Anastasia Baratta, Steve Garcia, Sue Westmoreland, First Congregational Church of Memphis, Gina Vestuti, Kelly Sicat and the Lucas Artist Residency Program at Montalvo Art Center, Deborah Bernhardt and Rahn Marion

Artwork in order of appearance:

"Still Searching" — Digital Collage, 2023
"Dream Glyph 1" — Yoga Class, February 25, 2023
"One Way, Begin" — Found poem in Lafayette, LA, late 00's
"Dream Glyph 2" — Dream, November 2022
"Dream Glyph 3" — Yoga Class, November 28, 2022
"Great American Eclipse" — April 14, 2024
"Broken Grails" — Overton Park, Memphis, TN — February 2022
"St. John the Evangelist (detail)", Museo Soumaya, CDMX — May 2017
"Dream Glyph 4" — New Moon in Pisces, February 20, 2023
"Camino Real Trail System as Constellation"
"Dream Glyph 5" — Date Unknown
"Dream Glyph 6" — Dream, November 2022
"Sister Juanita Leonard Carrying Her Cross" — May 2016, image used with permission from the artist, edited by Taj Chander
"Tunnel at Nambe Falls" — Sangre de Cristo Mountains, October 2019
"The Square Root of Victory — Yoga Lesson, March 24, 2023
"Dream Glyph 7" — Dream, December 2022

*a note on *Dream Glyphs* throughout this document:

These strange rune-like symbols began appearing in dreams and meditation during November of 2022—a lunar eclipse season occurring while I living as a resident artist in a church in Memphis, TN. The glyphs continued to appear in dreams and meditations throughout the following year, until suddenly ceasing. Later they were suggested to be off-planetary transmissions, sounds in the form of asemic poetry, documented for the reader's interpretation.Hundreds were recorded during this brief period. Their origin remains a mystery.

Taj Chander is an award-winning new age musician, film composer, sound healer and Kundalini Yoga teacher. His music has been featured in art and film festivals around the world including the Tagore International Film Festival in Bolpur, India; Festival Ecos-Urbanos in Mexico City, The New York Independent Film Festival, and OUTFEST Los Angeles. His work can be found on Bandcamp and streamed online.

www.ingramcontent.com/pod-product-compliance
Lightning Source LLC
Chambersburg PA
CBHW061704130726
47996CB00006B/2148